MY Heavenly ENCOUNTER WITH Mom

KATHY I. LESTER

WestBow
PRESS
A DIVISION OF THOMAS NELSON

WestBow Press books may be ordered through
booksellers or by contacting:

WestBow Press
A Division of Thomas Nelson
1663 Liberty Drive
Bloomington, IN 47403
www.westbowpress.com
1 (866) 928-1240

Scripture taken from the King James Version of the Bible.

ISBN: 978-1-4908-1049-2 (sc)
ISBN: 978-1-4908-1050-8 (e)

Library of Congress Control Number: 2013917802

Printed in the United States of America.

WestBow Press rev. date: 10/2/2013

DEDICATION

I would like to dedicate this book to my husband Rev. Daren S. Lester for his love and support for over 21 years of my life. Thank you so much for everything you have taught me and everything you have done. May God's grace and mercy rest upon you all of the days of your life. I love you.

TABLE OF CONTENTS

FOREWORD

I have had the privilege of having God place divinely appointed people in my life for the express purpose of revealing to me more of His divine Truth. Sister Kathy Irene Losey, who later became my dearest wife and is today proudly known as Sister Kathy Irene Lester, is one of those divinely blessed people that God has placed in my life for such a time as this.

God has chosen to relay to Kathy some of His holy hidden mysteries, and in doing so, Jesus has instructed her by the divine leading of His blessed Holy Spirit to share her brief, but exciting encounter that she was allowed to have with her mother, Bernice Irene Losey.

Sister Kathy's personal testimony of the events as they had happened gives us the readers a peek behind God's spiritual veil. Her spiritual encounter with her mother informs us of some of the daily aspects that our loved ones are engaged in since they've gone on to Heaven.

This book has been a real blessing to me and I am sure that it will bless and encourage you and any of your loved ones that have had a dear one cross over to their heavenly inheritance with our God and Savior Jesus Christ. This book should remind everyone that even though we on Earth may be temporarily separated from the ones we love here down below, we will also be soon reunited with them once we cross over there. They are waiting to meet us and we who are saved will be reunited with them for an eternal grand reunion with all of those who have gone on before us. Remember, as Christ lives, so shall we live. John 14:19 says, 'Yet a little while, and the world seeth me no more: but ye see me, because I live, ye shall live also.' (KJV)

And even though the mirror is darkened to us now, soon all will be revealed to you and I. I Corinthians 13:12 says, 'For now we see through a glass darkly: but then face to face: now I know in part, but then shall I know even as also I am known.' (KJV)

So, sit back, relax and allow Sister Kathy's spiritual experience to uplift you and bless your heart today. God Bless!

Apostle Daren S. Lester

PROLOGUE

I will be completely honest with you. I had no plans whatsoever to write a book, let alone have it published. It never even crossed my mind. Many of my family and friends in the North Country and here in Indiana would agree that I am not the chatty type (though close family members nicknamed me "Chatty Kathy" go figure, right?) but as I started talking with other people that could relate to my experience, I had many suggestions made that I should put it into book form so that others can relate, learn and compare their experiences with mine. People want to know about other people who have had out-of-body experiences and have visited Heaven or even Hell for that matter. I am the same way. It is something that I always wanted to learn more about and enjoy when people talk to me on what has happened in their lives whether it happened out-of-body or maybe in a vision or dream. I will tell you this. It wasn't something that I had thought up nor even knew what was going to happen or if anything was ever going to happen. It just happened. And it has changed my life forever.

I no longer have a fear of dying; I have had a couple of bouts with death over the last forty years and have overcome it all by the healing power of Jesus Christ. I am human though and I do kind of wonder about the sting of death just like a female wonders about giving birth to a baby before they ever experience it. But I know that through everything and anything, that God is in control of my life AND my death no matter what the consequence. I know Heaven and all my loved ones that have gone on before me will await me when it is my time to go. Through this experience, I have learned a lot of things about Heaven and I have yet to learn so much more. I hope and pray that this book helps you, heals you, gets you excited about being a Christian or becoming one, going to Heaven and meeting Jesus and all of your precious loved ones in the air. There is nothing better and nothing greater than this. Everything that the world offers couldn't and will not compare. It is so awesome and I hope and pray every day that you experience the power of God and His goodness and His faithfulness and His precious love for you. Be blessed!

Kathy Irene Lester

CHAPTER 1:

Life in the North Country

I didn't know anything different and knew of nothing better. From a newborn baby girl to a pre-teen, I grew up in a small country town not too far from the Saint Lawrence River and Lake Ontario. Having a French Canadian/Mohawk Indian descent, we were only ten minutes south of the Canadian border and lived off of a highway route between two neighboring cities in northern New York. It was an area full of tourism between the borders. People would come everywhere to see the different sites and attractions throughout our county. I was really blessed with the ability to take school field trips and Girl Scout outings to many of the places that surrounded my hometown.

It was an awesome, memorable time growing up as

a young girl in the early seventies and eighties. I have a large and happy, very close family with my grandparents and many aunts, uncles and cousins from both sides. My cousins and I were more like brothers and sisters than we were cousins. We never fought; we always loved to play together as children and were always excited when we came over to visit each other's houses with our parents. There were so many good times I cannot even begin to count them all. I love them all dearly.

And there was never a bad time nor a boring moment with myself and my next door neighbors. We were all close and had a wonderful time over the years. We were either busy climbing trees, playing with the farm animals or playing after school games in the pastures like 'Red Light, Green Light' or 'Red Rover'. On birthdays, we would stage talent shows outside by the garage doors and have our parents and other family members watch as we either sang or danced to the different vinyl records playing on my Mickey Mouse record player. It was so much fun!

I wasn't raised in a Christian home. I was born into Catholicism, but my mom, sister and I only practiced it on Christmas, Palm Sunday, Easter and Mother's Day. You know, the kind where you were born into a religion and followed it because Grandma and Grandpa and ancestors before that were in it and it was just something you were supposed to do. We went through the motions: Baby Baptism, First Communion in the first grade, etc… For a couple of years on Wednesday afternoons, I and several other classmates at school would have a half day and then be picked up by school buses and transported to Catholic Church school for the last two hours of the day. I cannot honestly tell you I learned very much. I just knew to respect God's house, do what you were told and don't make the nuns upset. I vaguely remember a few times that Mom took me and my sister to confession. I will be honest, when the priest asked what my sins were, I honestly didn't know. I mean, how much could a seven year old really do? The only thing I could think of at such a small age was maybe arguing with my sister once in a while. I never understood why that alone was a punishment for saying fifteen "Our Father's" and twenty "Hail Mary's."

I do know that in my mind and heart I had made an awful mistake when I was a little girl thinking that only people of the Catholic faith were going to Heaven. I am not sure if I had heard it from someone or it was just a thought I had put in my own mind. I ended up telling one of my Baptist girl classmates while swinging on the swingset at school that 'too bad she wasn't going to make it into Heaven like the rest of us.' Boy, was I sure wrong and apologized to her many years later since that day when we were adults. It is not a religion or anything you say or do that gives you a ticket into Heaven, it is a true and divine relationship with the Lord and believing and accepting what He did for you on Calvary's Cross so long ago. He paid a great price for us and for that I am forever grateful.

CHAPTER 2:

Searching

Enjoying the outdoors after school and during the summertime as a little girl was a never ending thing for me. That's where your imagination could run wild and you could do anything you wanted to do and be whoever you wanted to be. There was no need to have any technical gadgets to find things to do. You could make things up as you went along and time always seemed to have flown by no matter what I was doing.

A set of surrounding trees were used at times to border a play house, and a couple of rocks would be made into a living room chair. I'd have as many dolls as I could have lined up around different trees to portray I was 'raising a large family.'

There would be moments I would sit on the wooden swing that my Dad had made for my older sister and I which hung by two ropes from a large tree branch, and I would try to see how high I could swing into the heavens without becoming too scared. There were other times I would lay on the ground amongst the honeysuckles and gaze up into the sky to see if I could see past the clouds, and within them I would try to make out shapes and images before they would disappear into vapor.

I always wondered what it would be like if I could somehow jump as high as I could to see if I could reach Heaven and meet this God my church school had always talked about. There were many evenings I would come inside and after taking my bath, I would notice my mother sitting at the kitchen table with a Bible out reading through the Scriptures. For a long time, I couldn't understand it. Why would she be wasting her time doing that? She had plenty of books and magazines to read that she had subscribed to and some were even given to her by my grandmother. Why the BIBLE? I had asked her this once, but she always changed the subject by telling me that I needed to get ready for bed.

Well, my curiosity was killing me. So, one day I decided to take out my Bible that I had received from our local church and started to read. It was white with gold lettering and was encased in a wooden cedar box. I always loved the smell every time I opened it. I started out naturally on page one into Genesis and read every line moving my finger across each page. A couple of hours had past, and I was nearly halfway through the first book.

I didn't understand it. I thought it was so boring. Why would Mom put herself through all of this? I had decided enough was enough and put the Bible back into the cedar box and put it completely away. There was no need to read that old stuff. I was a good girl and a fairly happy one and I believed if there was a God, I did everything I was supposed to do so I should make into Heaven just fine. I didn't really know what Mom's worries were. She was a really nice lady and a great mother. Sure she had some faults and weaknesses, but don't we all? If you confess them to the priest, they would just vanish anyway, right?

Some time had passed and I had finally entered junior high school. I wasn't too thrilled. Going from a straight A student to barely passing each grade came from a result of me focusing solely on the peer pressure that continued on in school rather than my future and education. How can I make it to where everyone likes me? Should I cut my hair off? So I did. Should I borrow my mom's Jordache jeans and wear them to school? I tried. I knew one thing though. I wasn't going to smoke, drink, do drugs or have sex. There was no way I was going to end up with a bad future. So the bullying kept coming. But I never gave in.

It came to a point where I nearly had enough and became really depressed. I didn't want to go to school anymore. I didn't want to do anything. One evening, Mom had the TV turned on to a very popular worldwide Christian crusade and the preacher was saying if you were tired of what the world has to offer and wanted to try something new, then you needed to say this prayer with him, and make Jesus Christ your Lord and Savior. So, Mom and I repeated after him every line that he said. I had absolutely no idea what I was saying or what this would do for me. I didn't have any understanding. I figured after we were done, that God was going to come down like a lightning bolt and hand me a golden ticket to Heaven to redeem when it's my time to die. Or maybe a bunch of fireworks would go off above my head in honor of me doing something a preacher had asked me to do. Honestly, I don't believe my mother even knew what she was saying at the time. Nothing really had changed. We just did what we were told and thought it was the right thing to do. I was also hoping that would change my entire situation at school.

Things changed, but it wasn't better. It was a Friday afternoon and I was in English class. We were pretty much finished taking a test and we had a few minutes left before we would move on to the next class. There was a wonderful and beautiful young girl that sat behind me. She and I knew each other since kindergarten. She was mentioning to me that day that she was going to get ready to leave for the weekend to a youth rally out of town with her pastor and several friends. I didn't think it was a big deal, but engaged in the conversation. She had started mentioning something about 'the Rapture' and that she believed Jesus was coming back for His people. That everyone needed to be ready before the time comes. I had absolutely no idea what she was talking about. I just gazed into her eyes and nodded my head every so often. But I noticed there was something about her that was different that I wanted so badly in my life. But I couldn't seem to pinpoint what it was. Could this be in any relation to the prayer that I repeated from TV? What did I need to do to learn what she knew or have the excitement that she had? She seemed like such a sweet and happy person every day and all of the time. I knew I wasn't happy, but if you think you are doing everything right, then what else is there to do?

I didn't see this next thing coming. The very next day, bad news appeared across the TV screen. It was on local TV news stations everywhere. The van that carried my precious friend, her pastor and some of my classmates was hit by a drunk driver. There were several injuries, but the pastor and my friend didn't make it. From what I know, they were killed instantly. Our entire school was devastated. We were at a complete loss for words. Why was this allowed to happen? Nothing made any sense.

The school made preparations and gave permission to everyone that knew her to attend her wake and funeral. They even provided transportation via a bus route which I thought was very nice. I can remember after the funeral was over, and we all piled onto the bus for our ride back to the school to go home, how I just sat and stared out the window. I am not sure if it was a vision or a daydream, but I saw out the window a field of grass and flowers and saw my friend who had just passed running through it smiling and laughing. She was dressed in a beautiful gown. I can remember it like it was yesterday. She was at peace and I knew somewhere in my heart that she was home and in Heaven with her Lord just as she had talked about. The Bible says in 2 Corinthians 5:8, 'We are confident, I say, and willing rather to be absent from the body, and to be present with the Lord.' (KJV)

CHAPTER 3:

Giving Up, Letting Go and Holding On

It was nearing the end of summer in 1987 and things were going pretty good in our lives. Dad had just shared with us the exciting news that he was getting ready to pay his last payment on our house and was looking forward to saving up and buying things he and Mom had always wanted since he was nearing his retirement from his job. My oldest and only sister had already graduated from our local high school in June and took on her first job babysitting while driving back and forth in a 1980 Chevette that my parents had passed down to her to use as her first car.

Me? I was about to begin my freshman year after Labor Day weekend and was hoping the new change of going into high school would make the year awesome.

I was looking for something different. Maybe a new look? A new boyfriend? My old one obviously didn't want me back. Acceptance from what I thought was the 'in' crowd? Who knows? Anything would do at this point. I was tired of hurting and feeling like an outcast. I wanted to be somebody, but I didn't know what or who that somebody was. I figured everybody seemed to know but me. Change really seemed to sound good then. What I didn't realize is when the Lord has His hand on something and He has a plan for your life, change can totally mean something different than what you are thinking.

One summer evening Dad came into the kitchen and asked for all of us to sit at the kitchen table. Family meetings were not something that happened at all at our house, so I knew when one was called that it wasn't going to be anything good. 'I'm afraid I have some news to share and I need your help.' he said. 'We were informed at my job today that they are closing down parts of our plant and several workers and their families will have to make a decision to either take a small payout or transfer to the plant in southern Indiana...including myself.' My heart dropped. The room was silent. I couldn't believe what I had just heard. Indiana? I've never been out of state, let alone Indiana! How could this happen? What about my family on both sides? My Grandma? My classmates? My HOUSE? I would rarely ever see them or anything else again! This can't be happening! God, where are you now when

I need you? I repeated and prayed that prayer from TV. Why wasn't it working? Why aren't you listening? Help us!

'Dad, how much would the payout be if you took it?' I asked, hoping it would be more than enough for Mom and Dad to live on until retirement. 'Not enough to live on, just enough to get by until I found another job. All of my seniority would be gone if I stayed here. It would be like starting all over again. I wanted to talk to you all and see what you thought.' When he said that, I knew it was inevitable. 'What about the house?' I cried. 'Mom and I are going to have to put it up for sale while I am down south working. And then when it sells, we will move you down there along with all of our belongings.' he replied. Mom said, 'There's nothing else we can do but do what is best, right girls?' I didn't want to agree. I was mad at Dad's job, the world, and yes, even at God. What kind of change is this? I didn't want to leave everything I knew behind. Or did I? I was so confused. I wanted to run away. After several minutes, very reluctantly, I looked into Dad's eyes and said, 'I support you no matter what. It's not your fault.' Knowing he had the support he needed from us to make the move to Indiana, Mom asked if we would join hands and say a small prayer. What good is this going to do? I thought. I knew my life was already over... or was it the very beginning?

Time had passed and I had started my freshman year at school. Dad was in Southern Indiana working after he took down some belongings like clothing and other small stuff in his truck. My mom and sister and I would write him back and forth telling him how much we missed him, the events of the day and if anyone had looked at our house to consider purchasing. I was hoping inside that it would take until I graduated high school before the big move so I wouldn't have to go. Maybe by that time I would have a car, a job and maybe a place to stay. But it didn't happen. It was in December before Christmas vacation that same year that my parents had finally sold their house. My Dad had drove home to visit us around Thanksgiving and took not only another load home, but my Mom too so she could spend time with him for a few weeks down south until Christmas came. My sister and I kept up with house while I went to school and she went to work. Then in December, my parents had both flown back by airplane just in time to finish up Christmas shopping, spend time with us and family and then rent a moving truck until a few days before New Years Day in 1988.

Then it finally happened. My last day of school during first semester had arrived before Christmas break. It was also my last day at the school I had attended from kindergarten through the first half of ninth grade. I will never forget my bus ride home. I wished it would have lasted forever. I said goodbye to all of my friends and family that were on it and gave the bus driver a big hug goodbye. He knew me since I started school in kindergarten. I was in such shock I couldn't believe I didn't cry. As I was getting off the bus,

I turned around and stopped to wave at all the people I grew up with and cared for so much. Everybody was waving with their hands out the window saying goodbye as the bus drove down the highway. I turned around and stared at the moving truck while walking towards the basement door. This is it. This is really it. I am leaving New York and I am moving to Indiana. Everything I knew was going to be out of my reach. Literally 900 miles away. How will this all begin? Or maybe, how will this all end? I had absolutely no clue. Time passed as we had finally made the move down south. New apartment, new school, new acquaintances and even some new furniture. Yep, I hated it. I hated all of it. I felt like I stepped onto a new planet. We couldn't even bring my cat Precious for a while because the landlord said, 'no pets.' I missed her so much. I missed everything and everybody. How could God do this? What is the purpose for this? Doesn't He care about how I feel? Over time, after I had passed ninth grade and spent the summer pretty much alone, our landlord had asked if I had made any friends during the last semester. I really didn't. I had acquaintances and many of the kids that went to my new school came from the other school in New York from Massena. I only knew of one friend that I grew up with that was in my grade but we hardly had any classes together.

The landlord said that there was a youth function at his church close by and asked if I wanted to go. My parents loved him and his family, so they said it was okay by them. I will admit, I was really nervous, but once I got there I started to have some fun. The kids and people there were all really nice and included me in all of the activities. Was I dreaming? Was I actually going to fit in somewhere? Then it was time to go home. The next week had gone by and our landlord stopped by again and asked if I would like to go watch the choir practice their upcoming Christmas program. He knew I loved to sing and play piano so I decided to go. I loved it! After they had finished practicing, church had begun and it was a wonderful service. Towards the end the preacher asked if anyone wanted to make a public confession and would like to accept Jesus as their Lord and Savior. He explained what that meant and it donned on me. "So THAT'S what the TV preacher was talking about!" I wanted to make it right and immediately stood up and walked over to the altar. Within seconds, while I began to repeat the prayer with the preacher, literally almost a hundred people got up and walked over to me and started praying with me. It was awesome! I felt great and it felt like a black cloud was lifted from me. Yes, I still greatly missed my family and friends back at home, but something seemed and felt totally different. I was a changed person! I wanted to share it with the world and I knew definitely for sure I was going to Heaven because I believed, not because I was good. I had faults and weaknesses and I was a sinner even at the young age of fourteen. I couldn't wait to tell Mom when I got home. Boy, would she be so happy!

CHAPTER 4:

A New Beginning for Mom

I couldn't wait to get home and tell Mom the awesome news. I bolted through the door after I was dropped off at the driveway and started telling Mom everything that happened that night. My mouth was running like a machine gun. My mom just smiled and nodded her head and kept saying, 'That's good, sweetie. That's good.' I really couldn't understand at first why she wasn't excited as I was. Maybe she was trying to soak it all in? Maybe she thought I had eaten too many sweets before I left? Who knows? Oh, well! I knew what had happened to me and I was literally on cloud nine.

A couple of weeks had past and I had attended almost every service the church had. I was becoming a regular there and I loved it so much. One Sunday evening, I was getting ready to dress up for Sunday night and for Christmas choir practice and my Mom had walked in my bedroom. 'What do you think you're doing?' I looked into her eyes and drew a blank. Why would she be asking me such a silly question? 'Um, I am getting ready for Sunday night church.' 'Oh no, young lady. You aren't going anywhere,' she said sternly. I didn't understand it. What in the world has gotten into her? I am going to church, not a football game. What was she thinking? 'I don't understand,' I said softly. 'Well, understand this. You are not going every time the church door opens. You don't need to go three times every week. That is ridiculous, so the answer is no.'

I felt my heart drop. Why was she doing this? She has no clue what she is saying. Why was she acting like this? 'I am going to let him know you are not going tonight and you get into your pajamas and make sure all of your homework is done, understand?' she said. 'Yes, Mom', I said sadly. As I was changing into my pajamas, I started to cry. I just couldn't believe what I was hearing. What is so wrong about going to church and enjoying the presence of God? Why did she act so irritated and somewhat angry?

I crawled into my bed and began to pray. I felt so all alone and I was hoping this wasn't the end of my church going or relationship with Jesus. As I was praying, I felt peace in my heart. I just believed that tomorrow would be a better day.

A couple of weeks had passed and our landlord

had stopped by to talk to Mom about paying her to help clean some apartments for him. She did this from time to time and it helped her and Dad with the rent. He had also mentioned to her that Sunday evening, an evangelist was going to preach the beginning of a revival that was planned to last all week. He said he was really good and would like for her to come. I couldn't believe my ears. She said, 'Oh no, that's okay. Kathy can go, but I will just stay here and do some housework.' 'Mom,' I said. 'It would be so awesome if you would go. Just for one night. Please?' She looked and saw the pleading through my eyes. 'All right. But just one night. That is it,' she said. That suited me perfectly. I knew things would get better then.

Sunday evening came and I could not wait to get ready for church. Mom dressed up very nicely as she always would if she was getting ready for a party or for a wedding. As we walked into the church, the elders stood in a line on each side of the lobby shaking our hands with big smiles. 'This is my Mom,' I said proudly as we walked through the lobby shaking each hand. 'Bless you sister,' they said to my Mom. 'So nice to meet you. You have such a wonderful little girl here.' 'Thank you,' she replied and smiled.

We walked into the sanctuary and found a pew near the middle on the right hand side. Things were starting off well. The preacher started the service with the announcements. Then there was worship service. Then, tithes and offerings were taken. Then the evangelist started preaching and all of the sudden, the Holy Spirit came down. People started standing up raising their hands in the air to worship the Lord. One lady jumped out of her seat and started waving her hands in the air and speaking in an unknown language. Then the worship leader started to run backwards around the entire church with her eyes closed and hands lifted praising God. I was so amazed. But, Mom was not!

She whispered into my ear. 'We need to leave now.' 'Why?' I asked. 'Don't ask questions. I can't believe you talked me into this. We are getting out of here,' she commanded. As soon as she finished that sentence, the evangelist turned around from the pulpit and pointed his finger toward her and said, 'Ma'am, the Holy Spirit is speaking to you right now and you are being convicted from what you see.' She could not believe what he had said. How did he know what she was thinking? He started asking if there was anyone that wanted to accept Jesus Christ into their heart as their Lord and Savior. If so, they needed to come up and pray with him at the altar. After a couple of minutes, my mother got up by herself and walked up to the evangelist. I couldn't believe my eyes. My mom was giving her heart to the Lord! With tears of joy, I got out of the pew and walked up beside her as several others stood behind her and started to pray. It was awesome!

After that, her life had completely changed. Old things had passed away and all things had become new. She was no longer the same person. Everything she had searched for had finally fell into place and all of the puzzle pieces had fit together perfectly. Since that day, her whole mindset had changed. Did she start going to church three days a week?

Yep! She started going to church every time the door had opened and then some. She started singing in the choir, she eventually sang with me as well as solo and was put on a cassette tape that the church made. She took part in all kinds of ministries and even became a Sunday school teacher for many years. She grew in the Lord and became a strong Christian woman.

She eventually became my church secretary years later when Daren and I founded Country Hillside Church back in the early 90's. She helped us start the 'End Time Press' and helped us print publications and gospel tracts and we mailed them to hundreds of people all over the world. There were times of rejoicing in the Lord and life was good.

She really started living when my sister and I got married to our husbands and started having her grandchildren. She was so happy to be a grandma and had a great desire to share Jesus with her grandbabies. She wanted them raised up in the admonition of the Lord.

Life for her was beginning and it was anew and it wasn't ever going to end. She even started working in late 1996 as her first career working for a local restaurant chain and then later on became a store manager.

There was nothing she couldn't do when it was done all for the glory of God. Time had passed and the mid-2000's arrived and one day she felt something was completely wrong. Something wasn't right about herself. Not spiritually or mentally, but physically. Maybe it was just a fluke. Maybe she was just dreaming it up. But, how can you dream up a lump in your chest?

CHAPTER 5:

Jesus Evidence: Still Here, Still Near

I never saw this day coming. I guess nobody does. How can it be? I have heard it happening to everyone else's Mom...but mine? Why this cog in the wheel? How can someone that is a soldier for Christ be diagnosed with the nasty 'C' word? Yep. The doctors found the lump in her chest that she had found, and it was cancerous.

Over the next four years, there were chemo treatments and various trips to the doctors and the cancer center. Hair loss was evident, so she had to wear a wig. At one point, she had surgery to have her right breast removed and she was in remission for over a year. There, devil! She is back in action and all is well! With faith, all things are possible to those that believe according to His purpose in Christ Jesus. We got this! And she did. Life continued on as it were.

During that time, my Dad got gravely ill. Almost near death. He had suffered heart disease since the late 80's after we had moved to Indiana, and he had to retire early from his job in his early 40's. Mom's focus was entirely on him at this point. She didn't want to lose him. She stood on faith in God for her own health and nothing was going to come between that. After many prayers, the Lord prevailed and Dad got better and his condition was stabilized. Over that period of time, she didn't realize that her cancer had come back. Not only did it come back, but it came back with a vengeance. Without detecting it early she ended up with three more lumps, and this time the cancer had spread to her lymph nodes.

Then came the news that no child wants to hear. My sister contacted me and told me what the doctor found and said that Mom only had about six more months to live. What do doctors know? I thought. The 'just live by faith, and not by sight.' My God is greater than cancer. I bind this news in Jesus name. God wasn't going to allow Mom to die. She was still very young and had a lot of years left. She can beat this. It will all pass and we will look back at it and laugh because she will get through this mountain like she did before.

I can't and don't understand why but only the Lord knows. He sees and knows things I don't and He has everything in His hands and in His best interest.

She didn't last six months. She immediately went home to New York after she was told the news to visit family and friends one last time and said her goodbyes. When she had arrived back to Indiana, she went from car seat to walker to wheelchair in a matter of days.

Dad called me on a Sunday night in tears. 'Kathy, you and Daren and the boys need to get down here now to see your mother.' 'Dad, is there any way I could come next week? I have to work a lot of hours and don't know if I have enough gas to drive down there,' I said, not realizing how bad things were. He tearfully replied, 'I don't think she will even make it by the end of the week. She's dying, Kathy. She hasn't eaten in almost two weeks. The cancer has blocked her digestive system.' It felt like my heart stopped. Silence fell in the room. After a minute or so, I told him that we were all on our way.

When we got there, I was horrified to see her. This isn't my mommy, I thought. Who is this frail lady with the short white hair? She looked like she was almost ninety years old, not fifty-seven. Her right arm and legs were so swollen that she had to gain dress sizes to wear any clothing. When she saw Daren and me, she motioned for Dad to help lift her up so she could stand with her walker and give both of us a big hug.

After our hellos, Daren asked her if he could pray with her and she said yes. So we did. After God's presence came down, my Mom looked up weakly into Daren's eyes and said that his prayer was so beautiful.

After that, she would fade in and out. Hospice had given Mom morphine pills to ease the pain and relieve the starvation that her body was causing. There was a point that she thought in her mind that supper was burning on the stove and that she had to get up and take care of it. She tried so hard to get up from the recliner. We had to coax her to sit back down and told her there was no food cooking whatsoever and everything was going to be all right. Minutes later, she faded back out for the rest of the evening. There was nothing more that we could do that night, so we went home.

Daren and I drove back over the next morning and this time I had brought someone very special. It was my homemade yellow teddy bear that my Mom made back in the seventies to help me from having nightmares when I was a baby. She had gone to the department store, bought a yellow bath towel, shaped it into a bear that would fit my small stature, stuffed it, and sewn blue thread for the eyes and black thread for the mouth. Even with frays and pulls throughout his body and many 'surgeries' later, he was still perfect. That broken little teddy bear did a great thing for me as a baby and I wanted to give back to her what she gave me. Lots of love. I pulled the bear out from under my arm and said, 'Mommy, do you remember him?' She replied, 'Yes, I do.' I said with tears streaming down my cheeks, 'I want him to keep you company while I am gone. This is for you to remember me by while I am at work.' I placed the bear in her swollen arm and she had enough strength to stroke his head with her hand and say, 'Nice bear. Good bear.' She cuddled him gently and then fell asleep.

I know that a lot of times, the Lord uses things that are broken to uplift and give comfort. He can use things that have 'been through the mill.' That teddy bear went through a lot of rough times with me and was there when I needed him the most. It was time for that bear to help Mom. I prayed it gave her peace and comfort over the last few days of her life.

CHAPTER 6:

Be Ready

The time came. After a long four year battle to breast cancer, Mother knew it was time to be with her Lord and Savior. We never gave up the prayers and would continue to ask the Lord for healing in her body. We also knew that if it was time for her to leave us that she would leave following a heavenly host of angels peacefully and quietly at her home.

It was on a Saturday and we were all at my parents' house celebrating my nephew's 20th birthday. She requested that Dad not give her any medications that day so she could be aware of her surroundings regardless if she was in any kind of severe pain. She didn't want to miss out on this important day of her life to be with her family that she loved so much. She was unable to eat any of the party food that was prepared nor did she have the physical ability to sing

'Happy Birthday', but she made sure she had enough strength to get in her wheelchair so she could watch her grandchildren have fun in the family room one last time.

When it was time for us to go home, I gently hugged my mother making sure I wouldn't hurt her physically. I asked my mother what she would want me to tell the world for her should God decide to call her home. She weakly looked into my eyes and said, 'Tell everyone to be ready. Be ready to meet the Lord when it's their time.' That was the last words she said to me. Mother, it's been almost four years since you have left and I have not forgotten your request. Be ready, everyone. Be ready.

On Thursday, November 5th, 2009, my mother went home to be with her Lord and Savior. It was so hard not to cry at her memorial service but I did just as she had requested. She said it was a time to celebrate because she would no longer have cancer and she would be walking the streets of gold with Jesus and her friends and family members that have gone before. She told me not to cry but to rejoice and one day we would meet again in Heaven when it is my time to go. So, I kept that promise.

Time had passed and three weeks later things started to become a little more normal. Christmas was on its way and I knew my mother would want us to celebrate as if she was here. Normally and happily giving each other gifts, eating great food and having lots of fun. So, that is what we had planned to do.

It was three weeks later to the day on the Thursday that she had left. Who would have thought or known that what was to come was going to happen and happen to me? Was it a sign to let me know everything is alright? A promise kept long ago when I was a little child now revealed? I cannot explain it but I am here to tell what happened. I pray you read on…

CHAPTER 7:

Hunting for Christmas Lights

As I pulled up in the gravel driveway that evening after a long day at work, Daren bolted out of the front door with a big smile on his face. "Are you ready to take a small drive and look around at Christmas lights?" Although I was already tired of seeing the road after a thirty minute drive home, I smiled reluctantly and slightly nodded my head 'yes.' Since the beginning of our marriage, we made it a yearly tradition to go out a few nights a week from Thanksgiving Day until Christmas and look at Christmas lights and decorations on nearly every house in Springville, Indiana. Christmas is our most favorite time of year and to celebrate the season we had started our own traditions and still followed some old ones.

While we were traveling down one of the country roads, Daren turned his face toward me and asked, "So, what does my precious angel want for Christmas this year?" I really hadn't thought about it. After my mom had died and trying to get back in the groove of the normal routine at work, I really didn't think about anything else. I was still trying to accept that I no longer had a parent living on this Earth. I turned and looked back at him and softly said, "There is one thing I would like but only God could give me." Daren responded, "What's that?" I said, "I would love to be able to go to Heaven for a brief visit and meet my unborn children for Christmas. To be able to hug their necks and kiss their foreheads and let them know that their Mommy and Daddy love them. That's what I really want for Christmas."

Years back in the 1990's, I had lost a baby girl in between my oldest son Adam and my middle son Jordan. The doctor said I was five months pregnant when I had lost her. After my third son Justin was born, I have had several miscarriages throughout the years after I had a tubal ligation after the age of 22. After every miscarriage, I would have a dream of holding the baby whether they were wrapped in a pink blanket or wrapped in a blue one. I even had a miscarriage of a set of twins-one boy and one girl. I know and believe that each and every miscarried child are counted and named in Heaven. I also believe if a child has been aborted, they are there too.

We went back to the house and I prepared to settle down for the evening and get ready for another morning at work. Little did I know what was going to happen by the time I laid my head on the pillow that night. Moments later, it happened. My soul left my physical body. What was happening? I looked up and…

There she was.

CHAPTER 8:

There She Is!

There she was; my mother that I had lost three weeks before after a long four year battle to breast cancer. She was standing before me completely renewed, revived and strong. I truly believe that she had enough strength to carry large buildings on her back and fling them to the center of the Earth. God's power that had illuminated from her was beyond imaginable! She was dressed in a white, long-sleeved pantsuit with the hems covering her feet. Her countenance favored that in her mid-twenties as to when I was a small child but without any glasses. There were no signs of cancer anywhere on her body and no signs of having breast cancer surgery; she had both full breasts.

She had rich, glossy black, long curly hair that flowed past her waist. She had looked nothing like she did the days before she had passed. I had asked the Lord after the encounter why her hair looked so different than I had ever seen it before and He replied to me that He had 'given her the desires of her heart.' God gives us in Heaven the desires of our heart. He gives us what we desire to look like when we are at our best. I had known for years growing up that Mom would try her very best to make her hair really curly by spending endless nights with large curlers covering her head encased in a plastic slumber cap. Most days the curls would stay in really well but sometimes when the humidity was in full force, her curls eventually fell and her hair would once again hang straight. The curls that she had in Heaven were so strong and refined that there was no way her hair would ever fall straight. It was simply captivating.

We were both standing inside of a building. I cannot describe to you what the interior looked like because my eyes were affixed on her. Quite puzzled at first as to my whereabouts, I softly blurted, "What are you doing here?" I am sure she would have liked to reply with, "You mean, why are YOU here?" Instead, she smiled softly and said, "I am here to take you to see your unborn children." With great excitement, I questioned, "Where are they at?" She answered, "They are with your grandmother and great-grandmother. Come. Let me take you to them."

At this point, something didn't come into realization to me until afterwards is that I did not know that my grandmother, Marjorie, had given her heart to the Lord right before she had passed. I didn't find this out until I had confronted my father weeks later and he verified this to me. My birthplace is almost 900 miles north from where I live now so I was unable to be there at the time of her passing from death unto life. I already knew at the time I was little that my great-grandmother La Bar was saved and loved the Lord. I can vaguely remember years ago at an anniversary party that she had played some hymns on an old piano on stage. The whole room was silent and in awe of her precious talent that the Lord had given her. She had passed later on when I was 8 and my great-aunt had said that her last words were that she saw Jesus when asked whom she had seen when she was looking up from her hospital bed. She was a precious and wonderful lady.

CHAPTER 9:

Heavenly Cruise

My mother turned and walked outside the door and I quickly followed her into this vehicle-like structure. I cannot verify if it was a car, but it was silver in color with four tires and a steering wheel on the inside. When my mother and I both walked out the door to the vehicle in question, my mother got in the drivers side as I sat down in the passengers side. The road that we were driving on had looked normal but without any lines and I can remember the grass on both sides of the road were a very lush green.

At this point or at any point of the encounter, we did not make any kind of physical contact. Something was already in place of my spirit that if I was to do so, I would not have made it back to Earth and would have crossed over to the other side. I am not saying that is the case for anyone that has had these experiences, but at this time, that was the case for me.

As I was looking straight ahead while Mom was driving, I turned and looked towards her and said, "Mom, can I ask you a question?" She sweetly replied, "Yes?" "Do you know that you're dead?" I blurted hopefully thinking she was unaware. She turned her face towards me with a 'silly girl' smirk and replied boldly, "Kathy, we are more alive than you are." This statement that she had made was a confirmation in my spirit as to what my husband Daren was told by his late father and uncle when he saw them years ago after they had passed. It was the SAME exact statement. 'We are more alive than you are.' Is it because they are now in the presence of Jesus that they live? Are they living life to the fullest which means they are much more alive? One ponders on this concept on what is exactly meant with this statement.

Within moments and what seemed like seconds, we arrived at this very small white house. It looked like an older home that you would see on Earth. It had a front porch with windows and a side door that we entered in later on in the encounter. Now, I am sure many of you are thinking, 'Now, wait a minute. The Bible specifically says in John 14:2, 'In my Father's house are many mansions: if it were not so, I would have told you. I go to prepare a place for you'. (KJV) What do you mean you saw a SMALL home in Heaven? What about what Jesus said?' I thought about that myself once the encounter was over but God had spoke to me about it. Jesus said 'in my Father's house are MANY mansions.' He did NOT say 'in my Father's house are ALL mansions.' He said 'many', not 'every'. Even though we are not saved by works, we are rewarded by works in regards to what we have done here on Earth spreading the gospel and living for Jesus. Many since birth have done great things for God and shown Jesus in their life until their death. Then there are those that stayed babes in Christ until their passing. I believe the place that is prepared for you is determined on what you did on Earth for the Lord while you were alive. I do not know whose house that was that I had seen; but I know what I saw and experienced.

CHAPTER 10:

Family Reunion

As Mom and I got out of the vehicle, she said, "Before we go in, I would like to show you something first." She had gone before me and as I followed her to the side yard, I saw what had looked like to me a family reunion going on. There were people everywhere; both adults and children. I saw people standing and talking to each other both male and female. Some were sitting down and around what looked like a picnic table. I saw children playing in groups doing various activities. I did not see any elderly people. Does this mean that we all become youthful once we pass from death unto life? Is this part of the Lord giving us 'the desires of our heart?' I will be completely honest with you. I do not know of anyone who would desire to be old and feeble when they get to Heaven. Our desires are to have great strength and full of youth and vitality. Could this be an answer to one of our questions about Heaven? One may ponder.

Mom lifted her arm and pointed over to the right side and said, "Kathy, over here to the right are the Montgomery's." I want to note here that I personally do not know anybody with the last name of 'Montgomery'. My family who may be reading this now may eventually correct me here, but as far as I know, I am not related or affiliated with anyone with the last name of Montgomery. I am not sure why my mother had pointed this family out to me. I am sure there is a clear reason as to why but it hasn't been revealed to me as of yet.

She suddenly pointed to the left side with a smile and said, "And over here are the Lester's." This was my husband's family. My married name. I didn't know of anyone there that I had seen. On the Lester side, the adults were sitting at a picnic table joyfully talking to each other and I had seen small children playing; two were on a see-saw with one little boy that shared an image of my late father-in-law when he was a boy. As I looked down at him, he looked up and smiled back at me. He was dressed in period clothing relating back to the mid-1800's.

The introduction brought a special someone to my attention. I immediately asked with excitement, "Where's my father-in-law at? Where's Danny, Mom?" She looked at me and smiled and said, "Oh, he's here. He is just busy doing some things right now." I could feel a slight disappointment inside of me but wasn't concerned. I wanted to see him very badly. It had been 11 years since he was killed in a car accident on his way to work. Danny Jack Lester was a wonderful man who loved the Lord and his family. I am greatly honored and privileged to have met him and to be his daughter-in-law and to proudly wear the Lester name.

CHAPTER 11:

A Table Prepares Before Me

My mother turned to the right and had me follow her through the side door of the small, white house. After Mom and I had entered in, on the very right, was a large dining room setting where several people were busy setting the table in preparation of a great feast. It was a very long table with a white tablecloth and shiny white plates with white napkins. I did not notice any food on the table and no one was sitting at the table.

I asked my mother, "Mom, why is no one sitting at the table to prepare to eat?" She turned her head toward me and smiled and said, "It is not yet time. Come." She then continued to walk ahead of me.

I really do not feel that what I saw was the Great Banquet table. Could it be an individual family affair banquet where each family celebrates and rejoices being in Heaven together? Could it be everyone that you knew and loved on Earth meets with you at this special banquet rejoicing your death unto life in Heaven? These questions still remain in my spirit.

As we were approaching the end of the hallway, we came to a door that led to the stairway of the downstairs basement of the house. On each side of all of the steps was cardboard boxes filled with different items. I don't know if this represented that the individual that owned the house had just moved in and had not had time to unload the boxes or if it represents something else. All I can remember seeing was a bunch of file folders in one box and books in another. I don't remember what were in the other boxes. I do know I was thinking as I was going down through the middle of the stairway that I didn't want to trip on one of the boxes and fall down the stairs. My mother had no problem whatsoever and was always a few steps ahead of me.

As I reached to the bottom of the stairs, we turned to the left where it led to what I think to be a family room in the basement of the house. It was carpeted with a TV that was on but the screen was blurry and I could not see or maybe wasn't allowed to see what was on. I can remember pictures on the wall but cannot recall what the pictures were or who was in the pictures. I also recall a chair in front of the TV where one could sit down and watch if you were there longer than I was allowed to be.

To the left of the TV, there was a doorway that was engulfed in a pure white light. You could not even see the door trim or the frame of the door because the light had covered it. You could not see through the light or what was on the other side of the door. As I said earlier, my mother was a few paces ahead of me and had turned back with a huge smile and waved her right arm motioning me to move forward through the door. As I got to the door and started to put my left foot in, I was brought back to my physical body at my house in Springville where I had felt a tug on my left shoulder from my oldest son, Adam. I was back…

CHAPTER 12:

Where Am I?

"Mom, it's time to get up and get ready to take both of us to work," I heard Adam say as my soul met once again with my physical body. Adam told me that as I opened my physical eyes and looked straight up toward his face, I had this look of bewilderment as to not knowing where I had been or what had just happened for that brief moment. I stared blankly into his handsome brown eyes and was only able to creep out a small 'ok' as he walked towards the master bedroom door back out into the kitchen.

I felt like 1,000 lbs. as I tried to sit up in bed. I turned my head back towards my pillow and stared at the lump in the middle where my head had once laid. What had just happened to me? I felt like a part of me was still there because I could feel and literally see in my spirit where I was just moments before. Tears started to roll down my cheeks. I wanted to go back. I wanted to go back and I didn't want to be back on Earth. I loved my husband and my three sons but I knew at that moment I was really home; home in Heaven with the Lord. I knew in my heart that I still had a plan and a purpose on Earth that needed completion before departing eternally. I knew the reason why I had to come back but in that moment I didn't want to accept it at first. When you hear people say that the Earth is just a temporary place to stay; that we are only passing through, they are much correct. When you are in Heaven, you already have the knowledge and the assurance that everyone that you know and love on Earth is alright; there's no need for concern in Heaven. God still has His hands on your loved ones once you leave this Earth. Things changed at that point in my life and I knew that I would never be the same. A part of me was still there with my mother and other family. It is something that cannot be changed. It is now something I would not ever want to change.

While I was getting dressed into my office attire, I still had tears flowing down my face. How was I going to maintain my composure on the commute north and ahead for an 8 hour workday? Of course, I knew I would not have to explain to my office managers as they would figure the situation would pertain to the recent loss of my mother, but it was so much more. I couldn't suppress my emotions; I was excitedly happy yet sad at the same time. When you are in Heaven, you are at rest. You feel whatever you have accomplished on Earth is finished; the only difference being that I wasn't finished and I had to come back to Earth to complete the mission God has in store for me.

As Adam and I got in the car and headed toward his job for work, he quietly asked, 'Is everything okay, Mom? You look like you have been crying. And what was with that look you gave me when I woke you up this morning?' I turned my head and smiled at him through watery eyes. 'Everything is going to be just fine, Adam. I experienced something great last night and I am still trying to fit all of the pieces together. I will be all right.'

The conversation then became quiet and soon after we had arrived to his occupation. 'Have a good day, Mom.' Adam said with a smile. 'You too sweetie.' I replied as he left the car and walked towards the front entry. Now what? I thought. The tears started to flow again. I sure wish I could just turn the car around, go home and get into bed and just go back to where I was. But I couldn't. I had to get myself back into the routine of life and figure out everything later on. I asked the Lord to help give me strength while I was working and that I would be in touch with Him later on that evening for confirmation and provision on my recent overnight experience.

By the time I had arrived at the parking lot of the office building, I felt like I could continue the day and my emotions started to calm. Thank you Lord for answering my prayers today, I whispered out loud. God is always there for us and I had a sense of peace that my mother was indeed 'at home' with her Jesus. God is GOOD!

CHAPTER 13:

Closing Thoughts

What are your thoughts about Heaven? Have you ever had an out of body experience and had seen your loved ones in Heaven or perhaps Hell? Has the Lord given you dreams, visions and visitations throughout your Christian walk? Have you asked for them? Are you willing to receive a message or experience something from God? Think about these questions.

I have had many ask or wonder why I had this experience and I can only tell you from my spirit is that I continue to be open to what God has to say and His desires for His children. I can remember as a small child that I had asked my mother once to let me know what Heaven is like should she go before me. I remember her smiling down at me and replying with, 'I surely will if the Lord allows me to.' From that point on, I honestly didn't expect it. Maybe the Lord heard my desires when I talked with Daren about my Christmas wish? The Lord only knows.

I didn't see my unborn children that night but I realized in my spirit that it is not meant for me to reunite with them right now. If I had of seen them, I would have carried a greater loss home to me on Earth. I would have remembered faces, names and hugs and kisses. It would have tortured me throughout my life as I would greatly miss them and desire to be with them. It was best for me not to know anything until it is my time to go.

What next? I am going to continue to 'press toward the mark for the prize of the high calling of God in Christ Jesus.'(Philippians 3:14, KJV) I am not going to look toward the past, but I am going to head on towards the future doing all I can to reach souls for His Kingdom. Time is running out. Jesus is coming back looking for His Bride without spot, blemish or wrinkle. Are you ready to meet the Lord today should He come? If you do not know Jesus as your personal Lord and Savior, would you like to? John 3:16 reads, 'For God so loved the world, that He gave His only begotten Son, that whosoever believeth in Him should not perish, but hath everlasting life.'(KJV) Jesus came down to Earth willingly to die on the cross for our sins so that we can be with the Lord in Heaven forever. Acts 16:31 tells us to 'believe on the Lord Jesus Christ and thou shalt be saved and thy house.'(KJV) All we have to do is sincerely believe and realize that we are all sinners saved by grace.

What to do next is very simple. Sincerely ask the Lord to come into your heart and make Him Lord of your life. Let me pray this prayer with you:

'Jesus, I know I am a sinner and I have lived my life without you in it. I ask you today to come into my heart; fill me with your spirit, wash my sins away and make me clean and pure as snow in your sight. I ask you to become my Lord and Savior. I believe that you died on the cross and rose from the dead on the third day and now are seated at the right hand of the Father. I no longer desire to walk in the ways of the world but allow you now to direct my every path. I ask all of this in Jesus Name, Amen!'

If you have sincerely prayed this prayer, CONGRATULATIONS! You are now a child of God, saved and on your way to Heaven! These are such exciting times and the Lord is about to do some mighty things in your life. Tell me your good news! I look forward to hearing about it! I love you all and if I don't ever meet you here, I guarantee I will meet you in Heaven! God Bless!